RETRIEVERS

Some hints on
breaking and handling
for amateurs

by

B. B. RIVIERE

First published in mcmxlvii
by Faber and Faber Limited
24 Russell Square London W.C. 1
Printed in Great Britain by
R. MacLehose and Company Limited

CONTENTS

ACKNOWLEDGMENTS

THE author and publishers are grateful to the Kennel Club for their kind permission to include the Kennel Club Field Trial Rules in this book. The photographs for Plates 14, 15, 16 are reproduced with the permission of the Sports & General Press Agency. The photograph for Plate 11 was taken by Mrs. Riviere. Messrs. A. E. Coe & Sons Ltd., Norwich, have kindly supplied photographs for the remaining plates.

ILLUSTRATIONS

FOREWORD

I HAVE been asked by Mr. Riviere to write a foreword to his book. I consider this a great honour and it certainly gives me great pleasure to do so. Mr. Riviere has bred, trained, and handled his own Labradors for many years. Perhaps his best dog was Detmore Brandy—a very good dog. I so well remember, at a Kennel Club Field Trial, his getting a strong running cock pheasant just tipped in the wing. This bird went through very thick and punishing cover, black thorn and briars, and Brandy took the line a very long way and finally emerged triumphant with the pheasant, his face well ornamented with brambles. Yet some who criticize the Labrador say they will not face punishing cover. Well, Brandy could and would. Mr. Riviere has an intimate knowledge of his subject and I feel sure that his book will be welcomed by all those who train, or wish to train, their own retrievers. Personally I have read it with very great interest and wish it all the success it deserves.

LORNA, COUNTESS HOWE

HAWKRIDGE HOUSE
  HERMITAGE
    NEWBURY

INTRODUCTORY

THE association between man and dog appears to be as old as man himself and its origin lost in the shadowland before the dawn of history. So old is it that the love of man is now inborn and instinctive in all dogs, and his companionship necessary to their happiness. It is always a matter for wonder to me to see quite small puppies, despite the companionship of their own kind, crying and fretting for the presence of a human being.

By some of mankind at least this unique and immemorial bond is recognised and this feeling reciprocated, and to the happiness of many men and women the companionship of dogs is equally essential.

To those of us who have this inborn love of dogs, all field sports in which dogs participate, and their training for such work, naturally make a strong appeal, and whether it be a pack of foxhounds drawing a cover, a retriever hunting the line of a runner, a Welsh collie herding sheep, or a couple of terriers ratting in a fence, we get a thrill out of it. Apart from hunting a pack of hounds, which falls to the lot of only a happy few, there is, I believe, of all such sports in which dogs participate, none of greater interest, or which gives us a deeper insight into dog psychology, than that of breaking gundogs, and handling them in the shooting field. And of all gundogs, the Labrador retriever, with his in-bred natural ability, his keenness, courage and conscientiousness, will, in my view, give the best return for the time spent upon him.

When I ask some of my shooting friends why they do not break their own retrievers, the reply I usually get is 'I haven't the time or patience'. This is, I think, a mistaken view. If you are fond of dogs it certainly does not make excessive demands on patience. As regards time, if you have time to take your puppy for a walk you have time to break him, and on a walk is the right occasion to do it. If you are too busy to exercise your own dogs, a quarter to half-an-hour per day of actual 'breaking' is enough, nor need you worry if you miss one or even several days. A dog's memory is wonderfully retentive, and any lesson he has thoroughly learnt he will not easily forget. The essential thing is for your dog to have complete confidence in you as a higher being who is always right and whose word is law, and as a friend who will never let him down.

It is all largely a matter of common sense, each lesson leading on to the next, and all designed to further the dog's keenness for what he may do, whilst teaching him the self-control to resist what he may not. The whole thing may, in fact, be summed up in the one word 'control'—the handler's control over his dog and the dog's control over himself; and to establish this control without in any way blunting your dog's keenness, initiative and self-confidence is the whole art of breaking.

I cannot help thinking that if shooting men would try their hands at breaking their own retrievers, or at least acquaint themselves with the ordinary methods of breaking, they would handle them better out shooting. Although all breakers are out for the same end, the production of the perfect shooting dog and field trial winner, each, no doubt, proceeds on somewhat different lines to attain it. Some there are, I know, who prefer a dog which has run wild and unhandled up to six months or more. The methods described in the following pages apply to the less drastic procedure of educating and training a dog from its earliest puppyhood, which, personally, I prefer.

Maybe there is little that is new in these methods, but they have been evolved through trial and error over a good many years of breaking retrievers and are those which I find the easiest and quickest, and I offer them as the contribution of one amateur to this, to me, fascinating subject. If they help to put the novice on the right lines and possibly provide a tip or two to the initiated I shall be more than satisfied.

CHOOSING A PUPPY

In buying a retriever puppy to break as a gundog the first essential is to make sure that he comes of a first-class working strain, and the best guarantee of this is in the number of not too distant ancestors to be found in his pedigree who have won awards at Field Trials. So large a part does heredity play in the working qualities of a retriever that, in my experience, it is a waste of time and patience to embark on the breaking of dogs of a non-working strain.

Picking an individual puppy from a litter for working qualities, though a gamble, is not perhaps such long odds as picking one for looks. The qualities I look for in a puppy are friendliness, courage, activity and tail wagging. Almost all retriever puppies are naturally friendly, but any one not overwhelmingly delighted at the presence of a human being should be avoided. As regards boldness, the puppy least startled by a sudden noise and recovering his confidence quickest gets the highest marks. When the puppies are old enough to run about the one which moves most often at a gallop will probably be the fastest worker.

Tail wagging, I admit, is my own particular fetish, but I regard it as a most valuable quality in a retriever. A puppy whose tail is always wagging will almost certainly later on use his tail when hunting, which means that he will have an attractive style. Moreover, it has been my experience that when sitting still at a stand—partridge driving or covert shooting—a dog who expresses his feelings by wagging his tail hardly ever lapses into that most unforgivable of sins, whining.

COMING TO WHISTLE AND NAME

Coming to whistle and name is the first lesson to teach a puppy as it is able to learn it as soon as it can run. It is of fundamental importance as a dog which does not come

1. Told to sit

2. Sitting

3. Coming to the whistle

4. Walking to heel

'hell for leather' when whistled is no good to anybody. Fortunately it is very easy to teach, this being done purely by bribery. Always use exactly the same kind of whistle—I use three short blasts. Begin by using the whistle whenever you take the puppies their food. Thereafter, when the puppies are playing or hunting about and get some distance away from you, whistle them back and, as soon as they arrive, reward them with a piece of biscuit or other titbit.

Give the puppy the biscuit with your hand at a level which ensures his putting his head up to get it. It is even a good thing to hold it at a level which necessitates his putting his fore paws up on you to reach it. This will help him to a good delivery when, later on, in retrieving, he comes back to the same whistle carrying a dummy or bird. While the puppy is galloping back to you make a beckoning movement with your hand and repeat the words 'Come back,' 'Come back.' He will soon learn from this action to connect the voice and hand movement with the whistle, and you thus have two alternative methods of bringing him back without whistling, one of them quite silently. It is, I think, a good thing to continue the coming to the whistle lesson from time to time throughout a dog's career so that the response becomes almost an automatic reflex.

There is no better way of exercising retrievers on a walk than to drop them, *i.e.* make them sit, then walk on 100 yards or more, and whistle them up. It teaches them to stay put and to come to the whistle, and it gives them galloping exercise which they thoroughly enjoy.

Coming to Whistle and Name

To teach a puppy to come to his name exactly the same method should be used, except that for this he must be taken out by himself. If you are breaking several, a good exercise later on is to make them sit, put the food dishes down in front of them and call each by name to his meal. When your puppy has learnt his name always say it before giving him any order such as 'Sit', '"Hi" lost', etc. This is essential when you have two or more dogs out shooting and work each, as they should be worked, separately. Later on I teach all my dogs, by exactly the same method, as for whistle and name, to come to a 'hiss'. The sound carries some distance and is a most convenient and unobtrusive way of calling a dog.

WALKING TO HEEL

Walking to heel is the next thing to teach a puppy and he should learn it as soon as he is old enough to go for walks, which will probably be at about three months. The best implement to use is a rolled-up newspaper which cannot hurt him but which on impact makes a noise which he does not like. Choose as narrow a lane or footpath as possible for the lesson, have your puppy walking behind you and every time his nose appears in front of your leg give it a tap with the newspaper with a backward movement, saying as you do so 'Heel' or 'Come in', or whatever you like so long as you always use the same word.

At first use the lightest possible tap in case you frighten

him and make him reluctant to come on at all. After he knows what is expected of him you can be more drastic. He will soon learn to connect the impact of the newspaper against his nose with the word of command and, after a few lessons, will come round you and fall in behind when told to. In the course of time walking to heel should become such a habit that he will feel uncomfortable in any other position. Naturally a puppy should not spend all his exercise time in walking to heel but, between lessons, should spend far more in play and exploring on his own.

SITTING

It is as physically impossible for a very young puppy to keep still as it is for a young child. Though you may, therefore, teach puppies to 'sit' at a very early age, it is cruelty to try to force them to 'stay put' for any length of time until they are at least four or five months old. To teach a dog to sit, say 'Sit', at the same time raising your right hand and forcing him into a sitting position with your left. Continue this lesson from time to time until he sits down at the word 'Sit' and the raising of the right hand without having to be pushed down.

Having learnt to sit he must now be taught to 'stay put'. Make him sit while you walk up and down in front of him and then around him in ever widening circles, raising your hand and repeating the word 'sit' whenever he attempts to move. Continue this exercise until you can leave him sitting while you walk away 100 yards or more. You can then either walk back to him, give him a pat and tell him he may get up, or you can whistle him to you and reward him with a bit of biscuit.

The next step is to teach him to remain sitting when you are out of sight. Make him sit and then walk out of sight behind a tree or round the corner of a building, but not far enough away to be out of hearing. Keep him sitting for five minutes or more, while from time to time from your hiding place you say 'Sit'. After a few such lessons he will come to believe that even when you are out of sight you are still in control and that he cannot move without your knowing about it. When your dog is required to 'stay put' while you are out of sight, as in waiting for you outside a house, it is as well, besides telling him to sit, to accustom him to some additional word of command such as 'Wait' or 'Stay there'.

All these exercises are lessons in self-control essential to a dog's training and are useful in many ways, from keeping a dog out of mischief whilst waiting, to using him as a 'stop' out shooting.

When your puppy has learnt to obey the word 'Sit' he must be taught also to sit to a special whistle—the best, I think, being a long, gentle blast. That is most important, because unless you can stop a dog and make him look at you when he is out hunting you cannot direct him by hand signalling. It is also far easier to whistle him back after he has stopped than when he is still hunting. It is very easy to teach. All that is necessary is to give the whistle after the word 'Sit'. In a very short time he will connect the two and then you can omit the word and he will sit to the whistle alone. Practise him at this at increasing distances away from you, always raising your hand at the same time.

When he has sat down either walk over to him or whistle him back to you, in either case rewarding him with a piece of biscuit. Expecting one of these two things to happen will make him concentrate his attention on you and this is what you want.

HUNTING AND RETRIEVING

You have now a young dog who comes full gallop to his name or whistle, walks to heel, sits and stays put. He has in fact learnt good manners and is under control, but the serious business of his life to which all this is preliminary he has yet to learn.

I do not think it is advisable to start a dog on serious retrieving until he is five or six months old. That is not to say that I do not encourage my puppies at a very early age to pick up and carry a dummy or an old glove. And here let me sound a note of warning. A dog's idea of what is desirable is very different to one's own, and from the point of view of a Labrador puppy no more delectable object can be found to pick up and carry than some decomposing carcase of rabbit or rat.

Should your puppy appear with some such nauseating

object take it from him very gently with words of praise and on no account rate or hit him to make him drop it. If you do you will be laying up trouble for yourself by making him shy of delivering to hand when the time comes for him to retrieve.

As you have taught your puppy to sit before letting him retrieve there will be no difficulty in stopping him from 'running in' when first you throw the dummy for him to bring. A suitable dummy can be made by stuffing the leg piece of an old sock tightly with tow and tying up both ends and is better still if covered with wash leather. Make him sit, show him the dummy, which he is already used to carrying, throw it some 15 yards away in the open where he can see it, and almost immediately say his name followed by ' "Hi" lost', at the same time waving him with your arm in the direction where it lies. He will almost certainly immediately go after it. At the moment when he is picking it up give your 'come back' whistle, when he should come galloping back to you with it in his mouth and, on reaching you, should raise his head as he is accustomed to do when getting his biscuit. Take the dummy in your hand and hold it a moment while it is still in his mouth before very gently taking it from him.

The object of whistling at the very moment the puppy is picking up the dummy is to teach him a quick 'pick up' as well as 'come back', and this should be continued for a long time. After a few retrieves on open ground to show the puppy what is required of him always in future throw the dummy into 'rough' where he cannot see it but must use his nose in order to find it. The method described above should give your puppy a good natural delivery and prevent his acquiring that most irritating habit of dropping his dummy or game at your feet, or even further away before you can take it from him.

The reason, I think, why a dog does this is that he learns to associate your outstretched hand with having his game taken from him and simply anticipates what he knows will happen by dropping it. It can usually be cured by one of the following methods: When he comes back with the dummy put your hand down and pat him and stroke his head. He will, of course, have dropped the dummy as before and will continue to do so for some time, but if you persevere he will in time learn to connect your approaching hand with being patted instead of with the loss of his dummy and will gradually hold on to the latter longer, until you are able to pat him first and then gently take it from him. In addition to this, let him carry a dummy, bird or rabbit when walking beside you while every now and again you put your hand down and pat or stroke his head before eventually taking it from him.

Another good method is, when he comes to the whistle, to make him put his fore paws up on you to get his biscuit and to encourage him to do the same thing when retrieving. This is not an ideal method of delivery as a permanency but, after he has learnt it, a slight anticipation of his actually putting up his paws should give him the correct one. If your puppy holds on to the dummy too tightly, gently squeeze his underjaw until his grip relaxes. Should he acquire the habit of running past or round you, which with a very fast comeback sometimes happens, a few retrieves with your back to a wall or fence should cure this. An extra nervy dog which is still reluctant to deliver right up to hand and the jealous type of dog which dislikes delivering at all may be rewarded, after delivering, with something edible but this must be discontinued at the first sign of dropping the dummy in order to get the food.

It sometimes happens that a young dog which has had a perfect natural delivery suddenly develops—it would almost seem through 'sheer cussedness'—a bad one, dropping, walking round you, or putting his head down. Should this occur, knock off all retrieving for a week or two while giving him plenty of practice at coming full gallop to the whistle and putting his head up for a reward. As likely as not the next time he is asked to retrieve he will have forgotten his bad habit and will come to the whistle in the same way with the dummy.

When his pick up, carry and delivery of a dummy are perfect a dog should be given a few partridges or waterhens, and later on pheasants, to retrieve, the first few times with the bird's head tucked under a wing and the wings bound to the sides with string or an elastic band, which will teach him to get the right hold. Wild duck are not, I think, good things for a young dog to begin on. They seem to be an acquired taste and although dogs which have had much work at duck flighting often become keener on them than on any other game, few, in my experience, care much for them at first and some will even

5. A quick come-back

6. A good delivery

7. Two stages of good delivery

refuse to pick them up at all. Certainly a mallard drake with his long neck and rather exotic plumage is a somewhat disconcerting object to a puppy. Retrieving waterhens may help a dog to acquire a liking for ducks.

If your puppy will not retrieve duck or woodcock or snipe—and there are many who will not pick up those two latter—he can often be persuaded to do so if he has no time to think about it. Let him see you drop the bird, walk on with him some 100 yards and then send him back for it whistling him just as he reaches it. More often than not he will then pick it up in his hurry to come back to the whistle sooner than leave it behind.

Work your puppy at retrieving when he is first let out and keen and at the first sign of his interest waning, stop. Prolong the interval between throwing the dummy and sending him for it up to several minutes which will develop both his memory and self-control. Always say his name before '"Hi" lost' and wave him in the right direction.

Work him in roots, bracken, and all types of cover and encourage him to retrieve through fences and over timber, using, to make him jump, some special word of command such as '"Hi" over'. Old tennis balls provide a useful change from the dummy. They can be thrown much farther, are more difficult to find, and by their rolling teach a puppy to follow a line. The next step is to make him hunt for dummies or birds which he has not seen thrown and this he will do as soon as he has gained sufficient confidence that '"Hi" lost' and the wave of the arm indicate that there is something to find.

Hunting and Retrieving

As soon as the puppy is hunting freely a single short blast of the whistle—a sort of half-way house between those already learnt for 'Stop' and 'Come back' may be introduced for checking and making him turn if he is ranging too far, and the meaning of this he will soon learn. To keep him steady let him walk to heel while you throw birds, dummies or tennis balls in front of you and pick them up yourself as you come to them. Also make him sit whilst you throw these all around him, again picking them up yourself before, perhaps, letting him have one final retrieve as a reward.

This is the most interesting stage in a dog's training, as it now becomes possible to estimate what sort of a nose he has and how he uses it, whether he has the requisite 'drive' to face dense cover, and how he quarters his ground in hunting and with what sort of style. A good retriever should, in my view, hunt at a gallop, but must quarter closely and cover all his ground. The 'fast' dog which gallops straight out and straight back, except, of course, to a marked bird, is useless. A dog's instinctive method of hunting is to go a considerable way down wind, *i.e.* 'give himself the wind' and then work back, hunting back and forth diagonally across the wind, which is 'quartering'.

A good dog will not willingly go far straight into the wind for fear of getting up wind of what he is hunting for, and thus losing the scent of it, and it is interesting that this unwillingness is not based on experience alone but appears to be instinctive as it is noticeable in quite young dogs with little or no experience.

8. Delivery with paws up

If your young dog does not quarter naturally he can be taught by walking very slowly up wind, preferably in roots, and making him, by hand direction, hunt back and forth diagonally across the wind in front of you. It is as well to have, far up wind, a bird or dummy down, which he can eventually find as a reward for his hunting.

Style is inborn and cannot be taught, but every dog can be made to show the best style of which he is capable by fostering the keenness and self-confidence upon which it depends. The old idea that a young dog can learn from an old one is, I believe, a mistaken one so far as retrievers are concerned. Following a fast old dog will sometimes help to put pace on a slow puppy, and following an extra keen one in covert may give a youngster confidence in facing dense undergrowth but, apart from a few occasions with these objects in view, young dogs are, I believe, best worked by themselves. In my experience two dogs hunting together tend to get jealous and to race each other without using their noses, and are then far more liable to hunt live game and chase 'fur' than when hunting alone.

WORKING TO HAND SIGNAL

Ability to work to hand signals is a most necessary accomplishment in a retriever, as will be apparent to anybody who has watched a dog hunting hundreds of yards wide of where a dead bird is known to lie, with his handler totally unable to put him in the right direction. Having, in the course of his retrieving lessons, become accustomed to being 'waved' in the direction of the dummy he is sent to find, your dog will already have acquired the rudiments of this, but to get him perfect at it will require some additional time and patience. The method I adopt is the following:

With the dog sitting facing you 15 or 20 yards away send him to fetch a dummy which he has seen thrown or placed first to his right then to his left and then behind him. To send him for the two former use a horizontal wave of the arm in the direction he has to go, *i.e.* to send him to his left throw your arm out to your right and *vice versa*. To send him for the one behind him use an 'underhand bowling' movement, straight in front of you.

After he has had sufficient practice at this, let him have two dummies out—one to the right and one to the left, or one to right or left and one behind him. Send him for one or other by hand direction as above, stopping him by whistle if he starts off for the wrong one. In the course of time, longer or shorter according to his particular aptitude, he will learn to associate the movement of your arm with the direction in which he has to go until of three dummies, one on either side and one behind him, he will always fetch the one he is directed to.

When he is perfect at this, help him from time to time to find a hidden dummy by stopping him with your 'stop' whistle, while he is hunting and waving him in the right direction. This will give him confidence in you. It is very easy to over-break a dog to hand signalling, so that he gives up hunting for himself and relies entirely upon his

9. Working to hand signals

10. Working to hand signals

handler to direct him to where his bird or dummy lies. If your dog shows any sign of this knock off hand signalling altogether for a time until he learns to hunt for himself again.

HUNTING FAR OUT

In getting a dog to hunt far out for a bird he has not marked it is a help if you can associate in his mind some particular word of command, such as 'out' or 'get on', with going a long way away from you. Practise your puppy, when out for a walk, at going back to retrieve a dummy which he has seen you drop, gradually extending the distance he has to go up to 400 yards or so. As he is galloping back for it call 'Get on, get on'. Stop him once or twice on his way back with the whistle and when he sits down and looks back wave him on, again calling 'Get on'. In this way he will gradually learn that the words 'Get on', emphasised by the hand direction, mean to go away from you.

A useful variation of this exercise is to drop three dummies at intervals as you walk over a distance of some 400 yards and to send him back for each in turn, using the command 'Get on' each time as he is going away from you. At first he will probably forget about the third and farthest one, and possibly even the next, but in time he will readily fetch all three, which is also good training for his memory. Eventually, if he is keen enough, by using the same method, stopping him and waving him on whenever he is inclined

to turn back, you should be able to get him equally far out
to a bird or dummy the whereabouts of which he does not
know.

MARKING

Some dogs seem to be naturally good markers whilst
others are not, though these latter, if ordinarily intelligent
and keen, usually become fairly proficient with sufficient
practice out shooting.

The best way to teach a dog to mark, or improve his
marking, is to throw tennis balls for him, thus teaching him
to follow the flight of a ball—or equally of a bird when out
shooting—with his eyes and to notice and remember the
exact spot where it falls.   Begin by throwing two balls in
different directions and sending him, after a short interval,
for each in turn. As soon as he has learnt to mark the second
one accurately, use three or even four balls in the same
way and to teach him to 'hold his mark' lengthen the time
of waiting before sending him to retrieve them. Another
good way to teach a dog to mark is to make him sit, walk
increasing distances away from him to throw the dummy
and then walk back to him before sending him to fetch it.

The best mark I have ever seen made by a retriever
occurred in one of the Utility Gun Dog League Trials,
when the winner of the stake, a black Labrador, called
Solo, marked—from high ground it is true—a hen pheasant, which had carried on a good quarter of a mile before

coming down in a field of roots. The first dog sent for it had been taken by his handler into the actual field, but had failed to find it. When Solo's turn came, his owner-handler, aware that he had marked it, wisely sent him straight from where he was sitting. Away he went full tilt, across two fields and through a fence, straight as a die to the exact spot and retrieved it.

It was a most amazing performance, and how he kept his line I do not know.

Solo was a yellow-eyed dog, which supports a belief I have sometimes heard expressed that light-eyed dogs are, as a rule, better markers than those with dark eyes. Of this, however, I have been able to find no evidence among my own dogs.

WATER

A dog which will not retrieve from or across water is of very little use for shooting, as it is naturally the birds one cannot gather oneself for which one requires a retriever. In entering a puppy to water the essential thing is that he should take the first plunge himself voluntarily. The slightest suspicion of forcing or pushing him in may make him water-shy for life. For obvious reasons the summer is the best time to accustom him to water and one of the best ways to start is to manœuvre him, if necessary with the help of an assistant, on to the wrong side of a dyke or stream and whistle him back to you across it. When he has learnt to do this without hesitation you can send him to fetch dummies thrown both across and into the water. Practise him at retrieving dummies thrown or dropped some way out beyond the opposite bank.

There are few things more irritating than to see a dog which has been successfully got across a river to look for a bird lying some distance out refuse to hunt farther than the opposite bank.

I shall long remember a day's shooting in East Norfolk with a full gale blowing from the N.E. and blizzards of snow. Two pheasants, shot coming down wind, had fallen far out in an alder carr across water some 10 or 15 yards wide. Three dogs, shivering on the bank, had refused to go across, when one of the guns who had been walking with the beaters, arrived with his Labrador bitch. Although she had not seen these pheasants shot, this bitch, when sent, twice unhesitatingly swam the water and ranging far out through the alder carr on the far side, retrieved both birds, one of them being a strong runner.

I shall always consider this to be one of the best retrieves I have ever seen made.

When your puppy is retrieving from water always walk away and whistle him just as he comes ashore. This will prevent his acquiring the bad habit of dropping his game in order to shake himself which in the case of a wounded duck may result in its loss.

11. The right position for a retriever
at a stand

12. Evening Flight

13. Retrieving over hurdles

RUNNERS

Some dogs seem to be born with a natural aptitude for hunting a line, while others only learn to do so by experience or have to be taught. The puppy which puts his nose down and runs your line when he has lost you, will need little help or teaching in getting runners. Very fast dogs, even when they have learnt to run a line, are apt constantly to overrun it and it is only through practice and experience that they learn to cast back and pick it up again where they lost it. It is difficult to give a retriever sufficient practice on runners for him to become really proficient until he has had several seasons' shooting. I have known more than one terrier who could give points and a beating to most retrievers in runner getting. This can hardly be because terriers have better noses and is, I believe, through constant practice in following the line of rabbits.

A dog which has not yet got the hang of hunting a line and getting runners can be taught by trailing a partridge or pheasant for him, and all dogs can, I believe, be improved at runner getting by this method. To do this properly requires two people, because if you trail the bird by yourself the dog will probably learn to run your line and not the bird's. Tie the bird by the neck to the middle of a line some 10 yards long, make a 'Fall' by rubbing the bird on the ground and scattering a few feathers around, then, with one person holding each end, trail the line 100, 200 or 300 yards, making a few turns and leave it in 'rough' at the end, taking care in walking back to keep well wide of the line, so as not to foul it.

Show your puppy the fall and encourage him to hunt the line; this he will very soon learn to do, as the scent is, of course, far stronger than that from a running bird. For your brilliant runner-getter leave the trail for half-an-hour or even an hour before putting him on it.

Do not send a young dog for a strong running cock pheasant until he has had some practice with running partridges and hens. A tussle with a strong cock as his first experience may make him hard-mouthed with runners for the rest of his life.

RABBITS AND HARES

When I am breaking my puppies, I have one or more wild-coloured tame rabbits in a wire run adjoining the kennels which they can see all day from their own run. Later on, I turn one of these rabbits into a walled-in kitchen garden and walk about, accompanied by a puppy, flushing it from amongst the cabbages, and rating him 'Ware rabbit' if he pays too much attention to it. When he reaches the retrieving stage, I throw dummies for the puppy to fetch in such a position that he must flush the rabbit in retrieving them.

Being thoroughly broken in this way to tame rabbits of wild colour certainly helps to make a dog steady to wild 'fur', and blunts the sudden thrill and instinctive desire to chase when first he puts up a wild rabbit or hare from under his nose when hunting. Except for once or twice to make sure that he will do so, do not let your dog retrieve either rabbits or hares in his first season.

I well remember my feeling of despair when an eight-months-old puppy I thought the world of, and had taken out shooting (perhaps unwisely), chased the first hare he had seen, and a misguided sportsman, to complete the disaster, shot it just in front of him. It would be difficult to imagine a worse start for any dog, for in those few moments he must have convinced himself not only that hares were things to be chased, but that they were absurdly easy to catch! However, he was eventually persuaded to revise his views on the subject and subsequently won many awards at Field Trials.

On summer evenings I often take my dogs out shooting rabbits but hardly ever allow them to retrieve one. What fun they get out of it I don't know. They seem to enjoy it and it is good for their self-control.

PUNISHMENT

The modern retriever of any breed is a highly sensitive and conscientious animal, and to most a 'word is as good as a blow'. This certainly applies to the strain of Labradors which I have, any one of which can be rendered abject by verbal rating alone. I use simply the one word 'No' to warn or stop my dogs from doing anything they ought not to do, from running in, to hunting in the wrong direction or eating garbage.

Never give a dog an order without seeing that he obeys it, and, if the word is not enough and he continues to transgress, such as in constantly breaking heel, hit him hard enough to make him obey, but no more. This is better than constant nagging. Personally, I am no believer in severe thrashings for dogs and remain unconvinced that the benefit of chastisement is in direct proportion to its severity. So seldom do I have to hit my own dogs that I never carry the wherewithal to do so, and, if the necessity does arise, am usually reduced to using my hat—a soft felt one; although this may sound harder on the hat than the dog, I am convinced that its effect, in impressing upon him that he has done wrong, is as useful as anything more drastic.

If your dog has seriously misbehaved, go after him if possible, make him sit, and punish him where the crime was committed. Never beat a dog after he has come back to you; or next time, if he has any sense, he will not come back at all.

It may have been noticed that no mention has been made of leads, check cords and the like, and this is because I never use them. A dog must learn to control himself and if he knows he is controlled by a lead he will, I believe, be less likely to do so. If one undertakes the breaking of dogs which have already acquired such vices as running in or chasing hares, such things may be useful or even necessary, but their use otherwise is, I think, an admission of failure.

Punishment

To sum up it is obviously impossible to lay down a hard and fast rule for all dogs, which differ in temperament almost as much as human beings. A good rule is to apply the minimum of punishment which will effectually and immediately stop the bad habit or act of disobedience which has called for it. For a sensitive dog this may mean no more than a few words, and for a headstrong one, a beating, and in distinguishing between the two lies part of the art of dog breaking.

EARLY SHOOTING DAYS

Although I like to have a puppy well-broken to the dummy, and between nine months and a year old before I take him out shooting, there is no reason why he should not go to a few very small days at anything over six months, provided that his role is chiefly that of an onlooker. However intelligent and well-broken your young dog may be at home, do not be disappointed if he appears quite the reverse on his first day out shooting.

It is only natural that the crowd of strange dogs and human beings, together with the shooting, should disconcert him somewhat and make him appear absent-minded and unable to concentrate. As regards gun shyness, some of my best dogs have gone through a stage of being distinctly nervous of gun fire and have had to be introduced to it with some care, in order to avoid their becoming gun shy.

Even a young dog which has heard single shots fired quite close to him with unconcern may find the first fusillade he meets with at a partridge drive or covert shoot a bit too devastating for his liking. For this reason it is best to take your young dog to his first few shoots without carrying a gun yourself, when you can start him off some hundred yards wide of the line and work him gradually nearer, according to how he takes it. Do not, in these early days, let him retrieve any bird which he has seen shot or which lies in the open.

SOME HINTS ON HANDLING RETRIEVERS OUT SHOOTING

Spare a little attention from your shooting for your dog.

At a stand—partridge driving or covert shooting—always have your dog sitting or lying well in front of you. The majority of the birds you shoot will fall behind you, and, if your dog is tempted to run in, he will have to come past you, which may make him think twice about it and will give you time to stop him.

Don't let your dog retrieve any birds which he can see. It is the bird lying in the open, especially if flapping about, which tempts a dog to run in, but, if he gets it firmly fixed in his head that under no circumstances is he ever sent for such birds, he will in time learn to disregard them. Moreover, the proper use of a retriever is to find the birds which you cannot easily pick up yourself.

Some Hints on handling Retrievers out Shooting

Don't send a young dog to retrieve a wounded rabbit or hare, or a dog of any age if it means a course.

Don't send your dog for a runner which he can see until it is out of sight. If you do, it is fairly certain that sooner or later he will start running in to all such birds. Moreover, it should give you far more satisfaction to see him get a good runner by the legitimate use of his nose than by winning a course.

Keep your dog at heel when walking between stands. It is by no means unusual to see a group of guns walking from one stand to another deep in a discussion of war, politics, or the stock exchange, whilst their respective dogs, completely forgotten, hunt the hedgerows and range far and wide.

Don't imagine that even a perfectly broken dog will remain steady if badly handled.

GENERAL MANAGEMENT

The dog is a herd animal with a highly developed herd instinct and the worst punishment which he can be made to suffer is solitude. Through thousands of years of close association with mankind human companionship has become essential to his mental well-being and not even the company of his own kind can take its place. The more, therefore, one's retrievers are about with one the better it is for them and in my experience the more sensible and handy they become. When in kennels they should have the companionship of other dogs and an outside run from which they can see people passing and all that is going on. Whether a retriever can become wholly a 'house dog' without detriment to his working qualities depends largely upon the attributes of his owner's family. If these are endowed with plenty of 'dog sense' and can be trusted not to encourage or allow him to acquire bad habits he will probably be all the better for it.

It is perhaps significant that the dogs most subject to hysteria are those usually kept in kennels, namely hounds and gun dogs. In the ordinary house dog with complete freedom and the run of the house it would seem to be far less common. I am personally fortunate in never having had a case of hysteria amongst my own retrievers except in one case where a Labrador bitch who was for a time boarded at a keeper's, some of whose own dogs—as I learnt afterwards—were affected, had a severe attack immediately on her arrival home and obviously caused by the excitement of her return. She never had another attack, but for a week or two afterwards would not willingly pass the spot where it occurred and if made to do so would drop her tail as she went by.

In the two kennels of retrievers which I have known in which hysteria was most rife the dogs were housed in buildings, their only outlook being a blank wall immediately in front of them. Supposing that these dogs were exercised for three hours a day, and I should doubt if it were any more, their boredom during the remaining hours of daylight must have been extreme.

14. Walking in line

15. Judge and handler

16. At a stand

General Management

Suggestions—but little proof—as to the causes of hysteria in dogs have been legion, from dog biscuits to ear trouble, and it is now, I believe, the subject of scientific research by highly qualified experts. Meanwhile my own suggestion, for what it is worth, is that it may well be a purely nervous condition analogous to hysteria in human beings and what in medical terms would be called a psycho-neurosis. The occasions upon which an attack of hysteria would seem most often to occur are moments of excitement, such as when out shooting, when first let out of kennels after, perhaps, long hours of boredom, or in the case of my own bitch referred to above, arrival at her home after an absence. Is not this rather suggestive—as is the barking and yelping which accompanies the attack—of the hysterical human female who bursts into mingled tears and laughter upon occasions of emotional excitement?

That dog hysteria is 'catching', in so far that the sight of one dog in an attack can bring on an attack in another, is, I think, beyond dispute. Upon one occasion out shooting I saw three dogs in succession, all from the same kennel, sent to retrieve a dead partridge which was clearly visible lying out in a grass field. Each one in turn, immediately upon entering the field through a gap in the fence, fell into a fit of hysteria and had to be taken up. I was then invited by my host to try my own dog! Needless to say this offer was refused and the partridge picked up by hand.

Whether hysteria in dogs is indeed a psycho-neurosis or due to some other cause, the question still remains as to

why it has only made its appearance in comparatively
recent years, and to this it is difficult to find an answer.
Meanwhile, in the light of what little knowledge we possess
I believe that the best preventives are plenty of liberty,
plenty of work and occupation, and plenty of human
companionship.

It has been suggested, as mentioned above, that defi-
ciencies in diet may be a cause of hysteria. Certain it is
that many dogs live on a diet greatly deficient in vitamins.
Dog biscuits, for example, can hardly contain any. In what
now seems like the golden age, prior to 1939, this deficiency
could be made up with raw meat, brown bread, milk—
than which nothing is better—and even an occasional
raw egg. Cod liver oil is, of course, the best vehicle for
vitamins A and D. All puppies, from the time they are
weaned up to six months old, should have a daily dose of
from half a teaspoonful to a dessertspoonful, and unless
other vitamin-containing foods can be given, older dogs
too should sometimes have it. In the country most dogs can
supply themselves with a sufficiency of vitamin C. I am
often amazed at the quantity of grass my retrievers eat and
I have had several which have acquired the habit of eating
blackberries from the hedges when out shooting. Failing
these natural sources raw carrot grated over the food is as
good as anything. Meat, at least two or three times a week,
is I believe essential for a dog's health and in most towns
this can be obtained in the form of horse meat. Raw bones,
if they can be lured from one's butcher, are excellent. Every
kind of cooked vegetable should be given including

potatoes baked in their skins. These latter, broken up and soaked in broth or gravy, form the bulk of my own dogs' diet at the present time.

The diet of puppies comes, of course, under rather a different category. Puppies may be taught to lap at a month old or even earlier, the best method being to push their noses gently into a saucer of milk which has been warmed to blood heat by the addition of a little hot water and sweetened with sugar. If unsweetened they will refuse it. Soon after, stale bread crumbs or porridge may be added to the milk and at six weeks they should be eating good meals of bread and milk, porridge and minced meat, the latter preferably raw. They are best not finally weaned from their mother until eight weeks old. After weaning, the essentials in a puppy's diet are cod liver oil, plenty of fresh milk and meat—rabbit for choice—with brown bread, porridge, mashed potatoes and cooked vegetables for bulk. An occasional bone, raw if possible, keeps them amused, is good for their teeth, and is a source of calcium.

As regards the number of meals which a dog should have per day, as a rough guide I suggest the following: when first weaned four, one of them milk only, at three months three, at six months two, and at a year old, and thereafter, one.

Finally I am no believer in the frequent dosing with medicine, condition powders and the like to which some dogs seem to be subjected by their owners. If puppies are thoroughly and efficiently wormed at between six and eight weeks old and thereafter are properly fed and exercised they should ordinarily require no more medicine for the rest of their lives.

With regard to kennel accommodation the necessity for an outside run has already been stressed. The best flooring for this is brick, but failing this, concrete is, I think, the only alternative. It should be slightly sloped, with guttering and a drain to run off the water when it is washed out, and must be roofed so that the dog can be out in all weathers without getting wet. The inner or sleeping compartment should be well ventilated but free from draughts, with a wooden bench along the most sheltered wall. Owing, I imagine, to draughts at ground level all dogs seem to prefer to sleep above it, as may be seen from the house dog's constant desire to curl himself up on chairs and sofas, and for those which live in kennels a sleeping bench is essential. One suitable for retrievers should be 15 to 18 inches off the ground and from $2\frac{1}{2}$ to 3 feet wide. To keep the straw from slipping off, and for additional warmth in winter, a wooden board about 9 inches deep, should run along the front of the bench. This is best made to fall into slots at each end, so that it can be removed when the bedding is changed and the bench swept out.

FIELD TRIALS

The subject of Field Trials has been so thoroughly and admirably dealt with by the late Charles Alington in his

classic *Field Trials and Judging* (*Kennel Gazette*, 1929) that
I propose to deal with only one or two aspects of it here.

There is a class of correspondent to the Sporting Press
who writes—usually disparagingly—of 'Field Trial Dogs'
as compared with 'ordinary shooting dogs'. The former are
sometimes accused of being overbroken, and sometimes of
being too fast and keen for the 'average shooting man' to
handle. They cannot have it both ways. But I have never
been able to discover exactly what is meant by the term
'Field Trial Dog'. Is it intended to apply to all dogs which
have run in trials, or only to those which have won awards
at them? In any case it implies a belief that some definite
distinction exists between 'Field Trial dogs' and 'ordinary
shooting dogs', and it is time, I think, that this was dis-
pelled.

From my own experience, both as a judge, and as a
handler of my own dogs, during the ten years prior to 1939,
when owing to the war all Field Trials came to an end, I
can say that there were very few winning dogs known to
me over this period that were not habitually used as
'ordinary shooting dogs' by their owners between times.
Nor in my view could any of these dogs be regarded as in
any way unsuitable for an ordinary day's shooting if
properly handled. And surely this last qualification is not
an unreasonable one?

It has never been suggested that we should breed hun-
ters which can be ridden across country by those with no
knowledge of riding or horsemanship, or that Masters of
Hounds should be asked to produce a pack which can be

hunted by one completely ignorant of the art of fox-hunting and houndwork. But is not the demand so often heard for a retriever which can be handled by 'the average shooting man' getting rather near to the two absurdities suggested above?

There are, of course, very many shooting men who appreciate, understand, and can handle good dogs. On the other hand there are, unfortunately, perhaps as many who, though keen on shooting, take little or no interest in their retrievers and are totally incapable of managing them. If these latter must choose between having their dogs tied to them by leads or resting content with second-rate dogs, which will sit beside them half asleep and hunt for their game at a slow trot, it is surely nobody's fault but their own, and I think it would be a pity to try to eliminate the keenness, pace and drive essential in a first-class retriever in order to produce dogs which they can successfully handle.

The criticism of Field Trials most frequently heard from shooting men is that they are unlike an ordinary day's shooting, retrievers being asked to do at the former what would never be demanded of them at the latter, and in particular that, at Field Trials, dogs are to be seen careering about in root fields putting up game on fresh ground which has not been shot over.

This seems a perfectly fair criticism until it is remembered that the respective purposes of a day's shooting and a Field Trial are entirely different. The sole object of a day's shooting is to kill game, whereas that of a Field Trial is to provide tests for the competing dogs on which the judges can make their awards, the killing of game in this case being only of secondary importance so long as enough is killed to give every dog a full trial.

As regards the question of the flushing of game, the method of walking roots in line, killing birds as they rise, and sending dogs to retrieve them far out in front of the guns on fresh ground, is one, of course, never employed at an ordinary shoot, where such birds would be picked up by the beaters as they came to them, or, if by a dog, probably by one sent back after the fall had been passed by the walking guns.

There are valid reasons, however, for this procedure being so often adopted at Field Trials. On most shoots, roots provide the most suitable, and on some the only cover in which to work retrievers, and walking up is often the easiest and quickest way to kill birds into it. It is essential to test all dogs at walking up as well as driving, for to some the temptation to run is greater at the former than the latter. If a dog has to hunt for a dead bird, or to follow a runner, on fresh ground, as by this method of shooting he necessarily must, he cannot be blamed for flushing live birds, but his behaviour on doing so, and his ability to resist the temptation to deliberate flushing, provide a test of his education, and the control his handler has over him.

Another criticism sometimes made is that in spite of the supposedly high quality of the competing dogs, more birds are lost at Field Trials than at any ordinary day's shooting. In the first place I am confident that this is not the case, and secondly even if it were so, it must be remembered that whereas at an ordinary shoot, a large proportion of the birds killed fall on open ground, where they can be easily picked up, at Field Trials, for reasons which are obvious, all birds are dropped into the densest cover available. What would be the 'pick up' at an ordinary shoot if no birds were gathered by beaters or by the guns themselves?

The primary object of Field Trials is to test the working qualities of our shooting dogs, that is to say, their game finding ability, intelligence and controlability, so that the best dogs in the country may be known and can be bred from, thus improving the working standard of the breed as a whole. They also provide an attractive form of competitive sport for those keen on dog work, give amateur breakers and handlers an opportunity of pitting their skill against that of professionals, and enable any shooting man who has a good dog to try him out in competition with others.

An important result of Trials and the high standard set at them, has been the great advance made in the art of breaking in the past few decades, and a consequent all-round raising of the standard of education and control of gun dogs in general. Breakers can now get from any dog the best of which he is capable, and there are, I believe, at the present day, few dogs born bad. In the early days of Field Trials, it was not unusual for a considerable proportion of the dogs in any stake to be rejected for running in. In fact any dog which did not do so and was under a cer-

48

tain amount of control was almost certain of obtaining an award. For a good many years prior to 1939, 'runners in' had become something of a rarity.

Breakers of long experience are, I believe, agreed that retrievers are becoming year by year more easy to train. That this is due to careful selection through many generations there can be no doubt, and that the best medium for the selection is the Field Trial, must, I think, be admitted. Whether the qualities acquired through training can, contrary to what we are told by biologists, be transmitted, or whether what is inherited is only an 'ability to be trained' is a debatable point.

KENNEL CLUB FIELD TRIAL RULES

KENNEL CLUB FIELD TRIAL RULES

Copyright. Revised October 25th 1938

1. DEFINITIONS.—In these Rules and in any Regulations for the time being in force, unless the contrary intention appears:

(*a*) Words importing the male sex shall include the female.

(*b*) Words in the singular shall include the plural, and words in the plural shall include the singular.

(*c*) The word month shall mean a calendar month.

(*d*) The Committee means a duly constituted meeting of the Committee of the Kennel Club, and if and so far as any powers of the Committee have been delegated includes the delegated authority.

(*e*) Delegated Authority means a duly constituted meeting of a Sub-Committee of the Committee of the Kennel Club, or other body to whom powers have been delegated by the Committee.

(*f*) A Society means any Club, Society or Association promoting a Field Trial and its duly appointed Committee responsible for the executive work of the Society.

(*g*) A Field Trial is a meeting for the purpose of holding competitions for the work of dogs in the field.

(*h*) A Stake is a competition held at a Field Trial.

(*i*) A Nomination is the right to enter at some subsequent date a dog to compete in a stake.

(*j*) The Draw is the selection by ballot of the order in which dogs in a stake should compete.

(*k*) A Prize is a money prize or prize of any description won in a stake, other than a Special Prize.

(*l*) A Diploma of Merit is not a prize, but may be awarded at the discretion of the Judges at a Championship Meeting.

(*m*) A Certificate of Merit is not a prize, but may be awarded at the discretion of the Judges in any stake.

(*n*) The Breeder of a dog is the Owner of the dam at the time of whelping, unless a Registration varying this definition has been effected under the Regulations for Loan or Use of Bitch for Breeding Purposes.

(*o*) An Open Stake is a Stake open to all dogs of a named breed, without restriction as to variety, age or residential qualification of the owner, but it may be limited to a prescribed number decided by ballot.

(*p*) An All-Aged Stake is an Open Stake, but restricted by the regulations of the Society promoting the Field Trials.

2. REGISTRATIONS.—The following registrations must be made at the Kennel Club prior to the date of closing of applications for nominations or of the closing of entries if no application for nomination is required and must be made on forms supplied for the purpose and in accordance with the conditions thereon (All persons making any registration shall be considered as thereby agreeing to be bound by these rules and regulations, including particularly Rules 12 and 13):

(*a*) The name of a dog and the particulars required on the form.

(*b*) The last transfer of ownership of a registered dog.

(*c*) Any change of the registered name of a dog.

(*d*) Re-registration in connection with any error in a previous registration.

(*e*) A name assumed for competition or breeding purposes.

(*f*) The prefix or affix of an individual or partnership.

(*g*) The loan of a bitch for breeding purposes.

The Committee may decline an application for any registration or cancel any registration already made.

3. REGULATIONS.—The Committee shall have power to make, amend, or cancel Regulations for the following purposes:

(*a*) For classification of the breeds and varieties of breeds.

(*b*) For the registration of dogs' names, prefixes, affixes, pedigrees and other registrations under Rule 2.

(*c*) With regard to entries in the Kennel Club Stud Book.

(*d*) For conducting Field Trials.

4. STUD BOOK ENTRIES.—Any dog which has won a prize or been awarded a Certificate of Merit at a Field Trial held under these Rules, or Rules recognized by the Committee, who complies with the Regulations for entry in the Kennel Club Stud Book, is entitled to free entry in the Stud Book.

5. REFUSAL OF ENTRIES.— A Society may reserve the

right to refuse any entries they may think fit to exclude, without assigning any reason for so doing.

6. NOMINATIONS.—A person applying for a nomination renders himself liable for such fee or fees as are mentioned in the Schedule in accordance with the conditions stated therein.

7. PRIZE MONEY.—All prize money must be paid within a month of the date of the Field Trial, unless an objection affecting the prize money has been lodged.

8. OBJECTIONS—An objection to a dog must be made to the Secretary of the Society in writing at any time within twenty-one days of the last day of the meeting upon the objector lodging with the Secretary the sum of £2, which shall be forfeited if the objection prove frivolous. Should any objection be made which cannot at the time be substantiated or disproved, the dog may be allowed to compete under protest, the Secretary retaining any winnings until the objection has been withdrawn or decided upon.

Any appeal to the Committee of the Kennel Club must be lodged within fourteen days of the decision being given against which it is desired to appeal.

No spectator, not being the owner of a dog competing, or his accredited representative, has the right to lodge any objection to a dog or to any action taken at the meeting unless he be a member of the Committee of the Society, or the Committee of the Kennel Club or a Steward.

9. TITLE OF CHAMPION.—In each season there will be held a championship stake for the following groups of dogs: (*a*) Pointers and Setters, (*b*) Retrievers, (*c*) Spaniels,

other than Cockers, (*d*) Cockers, and the title of Field Trial Champion shall attach to the winners of these Stakes and also to any Pointer or Retriever which wins two First Prizes at two different Field Trials in Open or All-Aged Stakes, and to any Spaniel which wins three First Prizes at three different Field Trials in Open or All-Aged Stakes, where there are not fewer than eight *bona fide* runners in such stake, provided that one of the wins is in a stake in which, if otherwise eligible, a dog of any breed, age or variety of (*a*) Pointers and Setters, (*b*) Retrievers, (*c*) Spaniels, (*d*) Cocker Spaniels, (*e*) Water Spaniels could compete, and that at a meeting of Spaniels a win in only one stake shall be a qualifying win; the win to be in the Open Stake if there are both Open and All-Aged Stakes; but if there is an Open Stake for a named variety or group of varieties, the win in such Stake, if otherwise eligible, shall also count. The title of Field Trial Champion shall attach to any Bloodhound which is the winner of the 'Brough' Cup or of two Senior Stakes at Open Meetings approved by the Committee.

10. CHAMPIONSHIP STAKES.—The prize winners of stakes held to be eligible to compete in Championship stakes shall be decided by the Society under whose control the stake is run and the Society shall intimate as early as possible in each year the qualification decided on.

11. ORDER OF MERIT FOLLOWING DISQUALIFICATION.— If a prize winner be disqualified, the dogs next in consecutive order of merit, if so placed by the Judge, and

awarded not less than Reserve, shall be moved into the higher places in the Prize List and such placings shall thereupon become the awards.

12. SUSPENSION FOR DISCREDITABLE CONDUCT.—The Committee shall have power to inquire into and deal with any charge which may be made against any person (whether he has made any registration at the Kennel Club or not):

'For any act or conduct in regard to a Dog or any matter connected with, arising out of or relating to a Field Trial, or these Rules or any Regulations made under same which, in the opinion of the Committee, is discreditable or pre-judicial (or calculated to be prejudicial) to the interests of the canine world.'

The charge may be made by the Secretary on behalf of the Committee or Society, or by any person who is not suspended or disqualified. The charge, if made by an individual, must be accompanied by a deposit of £2, which may be wholly or partly awarded if the charge be dismissed to the person charged or otherwise dealt with as the Committee shall think fit.

The Committee, if any charge is proved to their satisfaction, shall have power:

(1) To suspend the person charged from taking part in or having any connection with or attending any Show, Field Trial or Working Trial.

(2) To disqualify from competition all Dogs owned by him or registered in his name as from the date when the charge was lodged and to disqualify from registration or

competition at the discretion of the Committee the progeny of any dogs owned by him as from that date.

(3) To disqualify him from judging at or taking any part in the management of a Show, Field Trial, or Working Trial.

(4) To reduce a charge under this Rule to a complaint under Rule 13.

The penalties above provided may be for life or such shorter period as the Committee shall fix, and the Committee shall have power from time to time to remove or modify any suspension or disqualification.

Any person suspended shall, during the period of such suspension, be not eligible to become or remain a member of any Club or Society registered at or affiliated with the Kennel Club. If any person suspended under this Rule shall attend any Show, Field Trial, or Working Trial, the Committee shall have power to increase the period of suspension and disqualification.

The Committee shall have power in any case under this Rule to publish the account of the same, together with the proceedings in respect thereto, in the official organ of the Kennel Club, viz. THE KENNEL GAZETTE, together with the name, description and address, and, further, to publish the names of such disqualified or suspended persons under this Rule, in two separate 'Black Lists', which they shall have power to forward to any person or persons concerned, as they may think fit.

Any person who shall employ any person suspended or disqualified under this Rule in any capacity in connection with Dogs will be liable to be dealt with as an offender within the meaning of the Rule, should the Committee object to such employment of a suspended person, and he may be similarly liable if he runs a Dog at a Trial knowing it to have been trained by a suspended person.

13. PENALTY FOR DEFAULT, ETC.—The Committee shall also have power to inquire into and deal with any complaint which may be made against any person (whether he has made any registration at the Kennel Club or not):

'For any default or omission in regard to any matter connected with or arising out of, or relating to a Field Trial or these Rules, or any Regulations made thereunder.'

The complaint may be made by the Secretary on behalf of the Society or by any person who is not suspended or disqualified. The complaint, if made by an individual, must be accompanied by a deposit of £2 (except where the complaint is against a Society for non-payment of a prize) which may be wholly or partly awarded if the complaint be dismissed to the person complained of, or otherwise dealt with as the Committee shall think fit. The Committee may, if the complaint is proved to their satisfaction, censure and/or warn any person guilty of any such default or omission and/or inflict on him a fine payable at such time as they may determine, and if the person makes default in payment he shall so long as such default shall continue be liable to be dealt with as if he had been suspended under Rule 12.

A complaint lodged under this Rule may be deemed to be also lodged under Rule 12 if the Committee so decide.

The Committee shall have the same power of publication as regards complaints under this Rule as are provided for in the preceding Rule.

14. DELEGATED POWERS.—The powers conferred on the Committee under these Rules, except Rule 3 (*a*, *b* and *c*), are delegated to the Field Trial Committee, but subject to a right of appeal to the Committee from a decision under Rules 12 and 13.

15. COMMITTEE THE SOLE AUTHORITY.—The Committee of the Kennel Club shall be the final court of appeal or umpire in all questions or disputes of any kind whatsoever arising from the competing of any dog at any Field Trials held under the Kennel Club Field Trial Rules, and whether such dispute be between two or more subscribers, or between subscriber or subscribers and the Committee or Secretary, Veterinary Inspector, or Judge or Judges, of such Field Trials, or between any or more of such parties and another or others of them, and any person or persons acting in any of the capacities above mentioned at any Field Trials held under the Kennel Club Field Trial Rules shall be deemed thereby to agree to refer any disputes which may arise between them or any of them to the Committee of the Kennel Club whose decision shall be final and binding.

16. FEES.—The following fees shall be payable:

Registration - - - - - 2s. 6d.

Registration (parent or parents unregistered)   5s. od.

    (*including registration of either or both parents if it be necessary*).

Registration (name not changeable)	-	10s. 0d.
Litter Registration - - - -		7s. 6d.
Re-registration - - - - -		2s. 6d.
Inquiry - - - - - -		2s. 0d.
Stud Book Entry - - - - -		10s. 0d.
Transfer - - - - - -		5s. 0d.
Loan or Use of Bitch - - - -		5s. 0d.
Cancellation of Name - - - -		10s. 0d.
Change of Name - - - - -		20s. 0d.
Pedigrees—Three Generations - -		5s. 0d.
„ Five Generations - -		21s. 0d.
„ Export - - - -		10s. 0d.
List of Wins (entered in Stud Book) -		10s. 6d.
Registration of Prefix - - - -		21s. 0d.
Prefix Maintenance Fee - - -		10s. 6d.

Holders of Prefixes paying 10s. 6d. per annum Maintenance Fee may compound on the payment of £5 5s. After ten annual payments the Compounding Fee will be £3. 3s.

Prefix Maintenance Fee (for Prefixes granted prior to 1919) - - -		5s. 0d.

Holders of Prefixes paying 5s. per annum Maintenance Fee may compound on the payment of £2. 2s.

Assumed Name - - - - -		£2. 2s.
Registration of Title - - - -		21s. 0d.
Maintenance of Title - - -		5s. 0d.

GENERAL REGULATIONS FOR THE CONDUCT OF FIELD TRIALS

Revised May 8th, 1936

DEFINITIONS.

(i) A Puppy is a dog whelped not earlier than the 1st of January in the year preceding the date of the Field Trials, but in any stake run in January a dog which was a puppy in the previous month shall be deemed to be a puppy.

(ii) Novice or Non-Winners Stakes for Spaniels, unless otherwise stated, are confined to dogs which have not won a First Prize other than in Puppy, Brace or Team Stakes prior to the closing of entries.

(iii) A Brace Stake is a stake for two dogs of the same breed or variety entered as a Brace by the same owner.

(iv) A Team Stake is a stake for three or more dogs of the same breed or variety entered as a Team by the same owner.

1. THE SCHEDULE.—A Society holding a Field Trial must issue a Schedule which is to be treated as a contract between the Society and the public, and neither party is permitted to make any modification except by advertisement in suitable papers before the closing of entries. The Schedule must contain:

(a) The date and place of the Field Trial.

(b) The latest date for applying for a nomination if such is required.

(c) The latest date for receiving entries.

(*d*) The amounts of nomination and/or entry fees and of prize money.

(*e*) The conditions for the Draw and for intimating acceptance or refusal of a nomination.

(*f*) A statement that the Field Trial is held under these Rules and Regulations with such exceptions and additions as the Society may mention, but no Society can exclude Rules 12 and 13, and Regulation 14.

(*g*) A definition of any Stake not defined in these Rules, or Regulations.

(*h*) The names of the Judges, where possible.

(*i*) The order in which the Stakes will be run.

2. COPY OF RULES.—The Secretary of the Society shall send a copy of these Rules to any applicant and shall have a copy with him or his representative on the ground during a meeting.

3. RECORD OF AWARDS.—The Secretary shall send to the Kennel Club within one week of the meeting a copy of the Entry Card with all the awards marked thereon.

4. RECORD OF ENTRIES.—The Secretary shall preserve all entry forms for six months after the meeting, and produce any of them to any official body inquiring into an objection or dispute.

5. APPOINTMENT OF JUDGES.—The Judges shall be appointed by the Society. When a Judge from any unexpected cause is prevented from attending or finishing a Field Trial the Society shall have the power to decide what shall be done.

6. NOMINATIONS.—If applications exceed the number of

nominations available, the right to a nomination shall be decided by ballot. If a nomination be not returned to the Secretary of the Society by a date specified in the Schedule the applicant will be held to have accepted it and be liable for the full entry fee, unless the Secretary can transfer the nomination to some other applicant.

7. REDUCING PRIZE MONEY.—If the full number of nominations be not applied for or nominations not accepted cannot be transferred to other applicants, the prizes may be reduced at the option of the Society.

The amount of Prize Money offered by a Society may be made to depend on the number of entries received.

8. ORDER OF RUNNING.—The Draw shall take place at such time and in such conditions as are stated in the Schedule, and at it each dog must be given the number that accords with its place in the Draw, and every dog must be tried in a consecutive numerical order.

No dog shall be called up for trial a second time until every dog in the Stake has been tried once. In Retriever Trials the dog with the lowest number under each judge shall be placed on his right. After all the dogs have been tried once, the Judges may call up for trial any dog at their discretion.

9. MANAGEMENT AT FIELD TRIALS.—The management of a Field Trial shall be entrusted to the Society, who shall decide any disputed question by a majority of those present.

10. WEATHER CONDITIONS.—If the Society consider the weather unfit for holding the Trials, the meeting may be

postponed from day to day until the end of the week when the stakes that are not decided may be abandoned and the entry fees returned; or a fresh draw may be made and a fresh date fixed for the abandoned Stakes.

11. HANDLING OF DOGS.—If a deputy handles a dog, the owner may be in the line but must take no part in the working of the dog. All handlers must obey the orders of the judges. Handlers will not be allowed to carry gun, stick, whip, shooting stick, or lead, whilst handling their dogs.

12. DOGS UNDER TRIAL.—The control of all matters connected with dogs under trial shall rest with the judges of the meeting, but they may call the Society to their assistance if they think fit.

The Judges are empowered to turn out of the Stake any dog whose handler does not obey them, or wilfully interferes with another competitor or his dog.

13. PHYSICAL CONDITIONS.—Should the members of the Committee present, after consultation with the judges, consider a dog is unfit to compete by reason of sexual causes or of any contagious disease or from an attack of hysteria occurring on the ground or any other cause which interferes with the safety or chance of winning of his opponents, such dog must be removed immediately from the ground and from the Trials. Any such case is liable to be reported to the Kennel Club and dealt with under Rule 12.

14. UNPUNCTUALITY.—A dog which is not present when required by a Judge may be disqualified by the

Judges or Society, or dealt with in any manner which the Judges or Society may decide.

15. DISCARDING DOGS.—No dog shall be discarded until it has been tried by two Judges unless it has run in or if two Judges concur that the dog is out of control of his handler or is held to have a hard mouth, but all the Judges must have examined the injured game before a dog is discarded for hard mouth.

16. CERTIFICATES OF HONOUR AND CERTIFICATES OF MERIT.—The Judges shall be empowered to give Certificates of Honour and Certificates of Merit to those dogs apart from the prize winners, which have, in their opinion, acquitted themselves sufficiently well to warrant them. A dog officially placed Reserve shall receive a Certificate of Honour or a Certificate of Merit at the discretion of the Judges. At Championship meetings this shall apply to Diplomas of Merit.

17. WITHHOLDING PRIZES.—The Judges are empowered and instructed to withhold any prize or award if, in their opinion, the dogs competing do not show sufficient merit.

18. WITHDRAWAL OF DOGS.—No dog entered for competition and once under a Judge at the Trial may be withdrawn from competition without the consent of the Society.

No competitor may leave the field without the permission of the Judges or Society and any dog so removed is liable to disqualification.

19. IMPUGNING DECISIONS.—Anyone taking part in a Trial openly impugning the decision of the Judge shall

render himself liable to a penalty not exceeding £5 at the discretion of the Judges, but subject to an appeal within one week to the Society, and further be liable to be dealt with under Rule 12.

20. QUALIFYING CERTIFICATE.—A dog which has won one or more Challenge Certificates at shows may be entered at a Field Trial Meeting, by permission of the Society, in order to obtain a qualifying certificate, granted at the discretion of the judges at the meeting. The dog must be entered on an entry form of the meeting, giving particulars similar to those required to compete in a stake. The qualifying certificate must be signed by at least two judges, that they have seen the dog and are satisfied that he fulfils the following requirements:

(1) Steadiness is not absolutely essential for a qualifying certificate; (2) that the dog has shown that he is not gunshy; (3) for a Pointer or Setter, that he hunts and points; (4) for a Retriever that he hunts and retrieves tenderly; (5) for a Spaniel, that he hunts, faces covert, and retrieves tenderly; (6) that where a test is possible for a Retriever, he will enter water.

21. CONTINGENCIES.—Any event not provided for in these Rules and Regulations shall be decided by the members present of the Committee of the Society, assisted by the Judges, and their decision shall be final.

FIELD TRIAL REGULATIONS FOR VARIOUS BREEDS

Revised March 13th, 1929

Retrievers

1. DRAWING AND COMPETING.—Before the Trials a number shall be drawn by lot for each competing dog. The dogs will be tried by batches accordingly during the first round. After all the competing dogs have been tried, the judges may call up at their own discretion any dogs they require further and try them again.

2. RETRIEVING FUR AND FEATHER.—All dogs running in Stakes other than Puppy, will be expected to retrieve fur as well as feather. In a Puppy Stake they will not be compelled to retrieve fur.

3. 'DRIVING' AND 'WALKING-UP'.—Where possible, all dogs should be tested, driving, walking-up, and in water.

Pointers and Setters

1. ARRANGEMENTS FOR CONDUCT OF FIELD TRIALS.—Immediately before the dogs are drawn at any meeting, and before nine o'clock on every subsequent evening during the continuance of such meeting, the time and place of putting down the first brace of dogs on the following morning shall, if possible, be declared. A card or counter bearing a corresponding number shall be assigned to each entry. These numbered cards or counters shall then be placed together and drawn indiscriminately. At the conclusion of each round the judges shall select such

dogs as they consider have shown enough merit to entitle them to remain in the stake, and a fresh draw shall be made among these dogs for the next round. When not more than six dogs are left in the stake no further draw shall take place, but the judges shall run such dogs in such pairs as they think fit, and place them in order of merit.

2. ORDER IN WHICH STAKES SHALL BE RUN.—The stakes shall be run in the order they are given on the programme unless the competitors, or their representatives, in the various stakes may agree otherwise—in which case the order may be changed, with the consent of the stewards of the meeting.

3. PLURAL NOMINATIONS.—When more than one nomination in a stake is taken in one name, the dogs, if *bona fide* the property of the same owner, shall be guarded in every round, where possible, when a draw takes place.

4. BYES.—A natural bye shall be given to the lowest available dog in each round. No dog shall have a second such bye in the stake unless it is unavoidable. The judges shall decide whether a bye shall be actually run or not, and if it be run, with what dog the competitor shall run it off.

5. ORDER IN WHICH DOGS ARE TO BE BROUGHT UP.— Every dog shall be brought up in its proper turn, without delay. If absent for more than a quarter of an hour, when called, that dog shall be liable to be disqualified by the judge or judges, and its opponent shall run a bye if required by them to do so. If both dogs be absent at the expiration of a quarter of an hour, after being called, the

judge or judges shall have the power of disqualifying them both.

6. REGULATIONS REGARDING HANDLING.—A person handling a dog may speak, whistle, and work him by hand as he thinks proper; but he can be called to order by the judge or judges for making any unnecessary noise, and if he persist in doing so they can order the dog to be taken up, and put him out of the stake.

Dogs must be worked together, and their handlers must walk within a reasonable distance of one another, as though shooting together. After a caution, the judge or judges may have the power of fining the handler the sum of £1, or of disqualifying the dog whose handler persists in neglecting this rule.

7. DOGS MAY BE REQUIRED TO WEAR COLLARS.—All dogs, when required, shall wear collars—the red for the dog with the highest on the card, whose place shall be on the left, the white for the dog with the lowest number on the card, whose place shall be on the right side.

8. COMPETING DOGS MUST BE SHOT OVER.—Every competing dog must have been shot over before it can gain a prize or certificate of merit, and satisfy the judges that it is not gun shy.

Spaniels

1. ENTRIES, NOMINATIONS, &C.—The Committee of a Field Trial meeting may make its own arrangements as regards dates of closing of entries, filling of nominations, and the conditions of stakes.

2. RUNNING OF DOGS IN SINGLE STAKES.—Dogs must be run either singly or in pairs, but not more than two dogs may be tried at the same time, even should there be more than two judges.

3. JUDGES MAY CALL UP ANY DOG.—After the first round of a stake being completed it shall not be necessary to have a fresh draw, but the judge or judges may call up any dogs they please and in any order.

Bloodhounds

1. ENTRIES.—Hounds must be named at the time of making entries, and particulars given in accordance with Kennel Club Field Trial Rule 2.

2. ORDER OF RUNNING.—At a date prior to the meeting, previously announced, a draw shall take place to determine the order in which hounds shall be run. By mutual agreement owners may vary the order of running, subject to the approval of the stewards.

3. QUALIFYING ROUNDS.—In the case of a large number of entries being received, a Committee may arrange for preliminary qualifying rounds to be worked off at dates prior to the actual meeting, when the hounds winning in the earlier rounds will be brought together.

4. DISQUALIFICATION FOR ABSENCE.—The Committee shall announce the hour for beginning each day, and each hound must be brought up in its proper turn without delay. If absent for more than half an hour when called, a hound shall be liable to be disqualified by the judge or judges.

Field Trial Regulations for Various Breeds

5. METHOD OF WORKING.—The Committee may arrange for hounds to be run singly or together in any numbers, provided the conditions are duly announced in the schedule. Hounds must be hunted by owners or their deputies. All hounds entered in any one stake shall be tried in the same way.

6. HOUNDS MAY BE REQUIRED TO WEAR COLLARS.— Hounds when hunted together shall wear distinguishing collars if ordered by the judge or judges.

7. CHALLENGE CERTIFICATES.—No hound shall be entitled to win a Kennel Club Field Trial Challenge Certificate unless he has clearly identified the runner to the satisfaction of the Judge or Judges.

Lightning Source UK Ltd.
Milton Keynes UK
UKOW050338131211

183656UK00002B/25/P